Evil Serial Killers

Inside The Minds of Psychotic Serial Murderers

Jane Corrigan

Table of Contents

Introduction

Before we can really begin to talk about the most evil and psychopathic killers the United States has ever seen, we first need to look at what it really means to be a psychopath. What is a psychopath and how are they actually different from any other murderer or even serial killer? Though the full answer is somewhat long and complicated, the short answer is that a psychopath is completely and totally aware of what they are doing and also completely and totally aware that what they are doing is wrong and they do it anyway. In essence, they don't care.

One thing that is important to note is that not every psychopath is going to become a killer.

That's because being a psychopath is actually a mental disorder and it's one that can affect a number of people without ever turning them into killers. To be honest, we don't know a whole lot about what turns a psychopath into a murderer, but we do know some factors that are used to differentiate an 'average person' from a psychopath and that's something to know before we get into discussing them at all.

Traits of a Psychopath

There are a range of different traits that a psychopath will generally encompass, so let's take a look there first:

- Uncaring – Differences in brain chemistry mean that a psychopath has no empathy, very little understanding of or reaction to fear and little to no perception of disgust. It's believed that this is because of weak emotional connections in the brain.

- Shallow Emotions – Social emotions are less developed, resulting in lack of shame, embarrassment and guilt. Even in times of intense stress, for example, they will show little to no fear in mental or physical reactions, resulting in a more callous appearance.

- Irresponsibility – Rarely will a psychopath take responsibility for their own mistakes, preferring to blame someone else for what they have done.

- Insincere Speech – While they understand the literal in words, psychopaths tend to have trouble with complexity in words, metaphors and abstract terms.

- Overconfidence – Overly boastful of their own abilities, psychopaths tend to have an over inflated ego and feelings of their own self-worth.

- Narrowing of Attention – Once they start a task, psychopaths are unable to change their path and will not be distracted by peripheral details, even in situations dangerous to themselves.

- Selfishness – Though they have difficulty expressing love to others, these individuals feel strongly toward themselves and feel their own wants and needs are more important than others.

- Inability to Plan for the Future – Have no ability to set long-term goals or follow long-term goals set by others.

- Violence – With an extremely low threshold for experiencing anger, psychopaths tend to get frustrated and aggressive easily and once there, tend to be overly irritable and prone to violent outbursts.

What Leads a Person to Become a Killer?

Probably one of the most commonly asked questions, when a new serial killer comes to light, is, 'what happened to them?' People always want to know if there was a sign that someone overlooked or if there could have been something in their upbringing that led them to this path. After all, not just anyone can become a serial killer or a psychopath, right? Well, that's actually two different questions with two very different answers.

If we're talking about what 'leads' someone to be a psychopath; it's actually not a question of 'teaching' at all. Rather, someone who is a true psychopath is born that way, not created after the fact. That does not mean, however, that they will go on to become a serial killer or a murderer at all. Still, someone can have psychopathic tendencies as a result of society, without being born that way. These individuals are more commonly known as sociopaths, so-named because of their 'social' upbringing.

When we look at what leads someone to become a killer there are a range of different factors that play a part. Is it possible for the factors in someone's life to turn them into a killer? This question is actually a double-edged sword. It is, in fact, possible that events in someone's life will lead them down a dangerous path, but someone who has had a life filled with all of the worst torments you could possibly imagine may go on to be an upstanding citizen and a contributor to the world as a whole. Someone who has had the most idyllic childhood and the most wonderful experiences in life can also become a serial killer or mass murderer.

The truth is there is no one factor in a child's life that leads them to become killers. Things like abuse, neglect or even mistreatment may or may not affect the children long term. Rather, it has to do with the child's outlook on their life, their perception of their own role in it. It's a psychological aspect that causes them to act out and to have less control over their own emotions and the things that they do. That's not to say they are entirely 'out of control' but that they don't know how to regulate their emotions properly and, as a result, they act out in an overly aggressive and violent manner.

Think about an infant who is not yet able to talk. When that infant feels hungry, what do they do? With most infants, they will start to scream and cry. They don't understand what they actually feel. They don't know that they are hungry. They don't know that they will be fed. They just know that something is wrong with them and so they cry and scream until that feeling goes away. In the case of an infant, that is until someone makes them a bottle and feeds them. Then they feel okay again. But at some point they will start to feel hungry again and again they will scream.

Psychopaths may have difficulty regulating their thoughts and feelings in a similar way. When something happens to them they become angry and upset. They don't know how to deal with the feeling like an average adult and so, they tend to act out in less acceptable ways. They may get into fights or arguments or they may hurt themselves or animals because they don't know how to regulate their own actions in an appropriate manner. They may feel that if someone angers them they are entitled to act a certain way. They also tend to have no understanding of what is appropriate or not. That means if they think about doing something, they'll do it, just because they want to.

An average person would think that if someone bumped into them in the halls they have the right to say something. Someone with psychopathic tendencies may think that they have the right to attack that person. It's not to say that their thoughts or actions are correct in any way, but it's the way that their brain reacts based on feelings of superiority and a lack of empathy for others. Sometimes these individuals are able to emulate empathy and they may get pretty good at it, but most times, even attempts at showing empathy will come across as awkward. Most times, people will notice the difference between true empathy and an appropriation.

The Homicidal Triad

Of course, if you've ever watched a crime show on television or in a movie you've probably heard about the homicidal triad. This is a trio of events that tend to showcase themselves amongst those who will someday become killers. These events are found in their childhood and have long been thought to be a precursor to future violence or sexual abuse. TV shows and even crime courses have continued to expound on the homicidal triad as evidence that a child will grow up to a life of violent or sexual deviance.

The triad consists of bedwetting, cruelty to animals and fire-starting and was originally established by a forensic psychiatrist known as MacDonald. In 1963, he published a paper on this triad based on his experience with the Colorado Psychopathic Hospital in Denver where he worked with approximately 100 patients. His 'triad' however, actually contained two other aspects, 'extreme maternal seduction' and 'great parental brutality.'

With the patients he interviewed and treated, MacDonald found that these traits were extremely common and so his published paper expounded a theory that they were actually precursors to deviant behavior in the future. He believed if a child displaying these traits could be found earlier, their potential for danger could be reduced. However, the research that he conducted was not as conclusive as he first thought and even he eventually found that there was much about the theory that couldn't be proven on a larger scale. As such, though the theory has continued to be touted just about everywhere, it's not truly a determining factor of what may happen in the future. Instead it's something that requires a great deal more research.

When push comes to shove, there's really no way that we can predict if someone will become a serial killer. There are no tell-tale signs in their childhood that say they will someday go on to hurt others. There are no tell-tale signs in their brain that definitively say they will go on to hurt others. Though research and science are starting to discover the precursors of psychopathic and sociopathic tendencies in the brain, even these signs do not guarantee any specific result.

It's important to note that, someone with psychopathic or sociopathic tendencies may live a relatively normal life and avoid harm to others. Someone with an awful childhood of abuse and neglect can go on to become an excellent member of society, such as Oprah Winfrey and Nicki Minaj. On the other hand, someone with an excellent childhood could become the worst serial killer we've ever heard of, like Jeffrey Dahmer and Dennis Rader. In short, there's no telling what someone could do in their life, and that's never more apparent than right here, with these nine horrible serial killers, who encompass some of the best and worst pasts you could imagine.

Chapter I: Ted Bundy

Just about everyone has heard of Ted Bundy, though not everyone really knows the true story about who he was and what he did. Rather, people mostly know him only as a serial killer and possibly as one of the few who was able to escape the police (and not just once but actually twice). But of course, as with anyone, there's more to the story than what anyone actually knows. For Ted Bundy, the story of his childhood is one that could make him a poster child for dysfunction and crime. Unfortunately, Ted Bundy lived down to the stereotypes that could have been set by his upbringing, and nothing would ever be 'normal' for him.

It was 1946 when Theodore Cowell was born to an unwed mother and an unknown father. Eleanor wasn't sure what to do with the child that everyone wanted her to get rid of, but she also wasn't sure she wanted to abide by their wishes. So she brought little Ted home to live with her parents, who informally adopted the child, leading him to believe, for the next several years of his life, that they were his parents and Eleanor, his sister.

Eleanor listed a young Air Force veteran named Lloyd Marshal as Ted's father, but later she claimed the man was actually Jack Worthington, a sailor who had managed to seduce her. Unfortunately, for Ted, neither man was ever proven to be his father nor records would actually never prove that Jack

Worthington even existed let along had crossed paths with Eleanor. As a result, Ted never knew his biological father, though cycles of documented abuse and commentary led many to believe that his grandfather may well have been the biological father and the main reason that his mother never identified a real one.

In fact, Ted, his mother and his grandmother were said to have been abused by his grandfather, though his grandmother was also said to be mentally ill, which led to her being subjected to electroshock treatments. His life went on this way for several years, but things changed slightly for Ted when he was about five years old and his mother married Johnny Bundy, the man whose name he would later take and the start of his understanding about his heritage. Throughout his schooling there was little to suggest that Ted would go on to become a serial killer and mass murderer. Rather, he was somewhat isolated but not altogether disliked by his peers.

Still, Ted was violent, obsessed with material things and known to make up stories and lies to hide the truth about his new stepfathers respectable, but meager, way of life. As a young adult Ted even managed to work at a Suicide Hotline, though it was only three years later that he is believed by some to have attempted his first murder. Of course, that's only if you don't believe what many do, that his first murder was carried out long before graduation, long before law school, at a time when Ted Bundy was only 15 years old himself and his victim only 10.

No one is really certain about the little girl and even Ted Bundy has never admitted to her death (though his mother vehemently denies it). It's believed that his very first victim could have been a neighbor when he was only 15 years old. The child was 10 years old the night she went missing and had been seen only a short time before. In fact, she was seen in the middle of the night informing her parents that her younger sister was sick, but vanished before the next morning when her parents woke up. A nearby acquaintance who had been completely obsessed with her local paperboy, Bundy is believed to have possibly gotten tired of her obsession or simply decided to graduate from the smaller crimes he participated in. But when she disappeared there was never a body found and though he was questioned several times after his arrest, Bundy refused to speak about her.

He was 19 when he started to truly come into his own, attacking for the first time on a university campus, a place he would go on to kills many more young women. But one of these girls managed to survive. Only one would die that night, having been bludgeoned with a piece of wood all the way to her death. The second girl, Lisa, managed to survive the terrible ordeal and her share of the horrible beating, but she suffered blows to the head that rendered her memory unsalvageable and though she would live, she would never remember what happened or who was responsible.

It was six more years before another female body would surface with similar wounds and brutality. Found in the Seattle area, the girl actually lived in a house filled with people and at the time she was murdered there were many others in the home, but having retreated to the basement for time alone, no one noticed until over a day that she hadn't been seen. Going to investigate led to a gruesome sight where the girl had been savagely beaten with what appeared to be a metal rod from her bed, which had then been shoved into her vagina. Even though it had taken so long for her to be found, the girl would actually survive the horrific attack, left with extreme brain damage and internal organ damage, she too would have no memory of the horrible attack she suffered.

The first girl Bundy would ever admit to killing would come later. 21-year-old Lynda Healy vanished with no one the wiser, though she had been seen entering her room that very night. It wasn't until police searched her room that they would find the massive amount of blood hiding under her neatly made blankets. Her skull was the only thing that anyone ever found of the woman and even just that small piece showed signs of a savage amount of beating.

No one truly knows how many victims Ted Bundy had because he never actually admitted to them all. In fact, he only ever admitted to 36 killings, but it's believed that the number is far greater. What is known is that his victims were all female, whether girls or young women and they were murdered during the 1970's. The location, however, is extremely varied, as Ted Bundy would go on to travel into different parts of the country while he was in the midst of his killing spree, murdering women from Washington and Colorado to Florida, Idaho and Vermont before finally being caught.

It was partially because of his charisma that Bundy was able to go on for so long with his killing spree. Able to kidnap women from public places with no one the wiser, he would often use a ruse of faking an injury to make the women more comfortable and compliant when he lured them away. They would feel safe and in control, right up until he would hit them with something and drive off with them in the back of his car to do whatever he wanted with.

That's because, when he had managed to lure the women away from public and away from potential help he would take them to a secluded place where he would sexually assault them. When he was finished with them he would kill them in any of a number of ways, though he would generally torture them by beatings and other assaults before he killed them. Some of the women he even decapitated, bringing 12 of their heads back to his apartment where he kept them until his capture. That, however, wouldn't occur until 1978, 6 years after his first suspected murder.

It was 1977 when Bundy was first arrested for murder in Colorado. An extremely smart man, however, he was able to escape for the first time while on trial. Of course, this wouldn't be the last time that Bundy was arrested and managed to evade his captors. He would do it again six months later, this time from a jail. It would then be another two months before he would again be arrested in February of 1978. Between his captures however, he was able to brutally attack yet another set of girls, this time on a university campus where three were killed and two were horribly injured. All were beaten with a blunt object, as was standard for Bundy in his kills.

If it seemed to take a long time before Bundy was actually charged and sentenced to death by electric chair, the time it would take before he would actually be put to death would seem far longer. It would take nearly a decade before his sentence would actually be carried out.

Even more strange, his estranged mother would continue to stand by him throughout his trial and beyond, insisting that he would never have killed or injured the women he'd been accused of murdering. It wasn't until his confession while on death row that she would ever admit that he could have done such a thing, and even after she would talk of his good qualities and the fact that he would never have hurt a child, especially when so young himself, as many believed his first victim to have been a 10-year-old girl.

In 1989, Ted Bundy was killed by electric chair for the murders of Lisa Levy, Margaret Bowman and Kimberly Leach.

Chapter II: John Wayne Gacy

Another extremely popular name in the way of criminals and serial murderers is John Wayne Gacy. Known for murdering over 30 teen boys and men, Gacy had the quintessential troubled upbringing of a criminal mastermind. With a life characterized by pain and suffering, Gacy would go on to become one of the worst serial killers known in the United States. But there is much more to his story than most people ever know and a whole lot you'll want to know about just how he managed to continue his reign of terror for so long, undetected.

John Wayne Gacy was born in 1942 in Chicago, Illinois. With parents who were Danish and Polish, he was one of several siblings who were all abused by their father. A drunk who would physically assault the mother as well as beating the children with razor straps, Gacy would find himself the brunt of his father's anger more than the rest. Gacy suffered from a congenital heart condition that made him weaker than the other children, though he would never own up to the weakness. His father, however, would see the deformity as something to be ashamed of and would always look down on him for it.

As he started to grow older Gacy came to realize that he was gay and began to feel even further torn about himself and his feelings. This may have been yet another aspect of his life that led to his future killing. After being tortured and tormented by his own father for each minor infraction, his beliefs about himself as part of his sexuality were most definitely dangerous and difficult for him to understand. It meant a great deal of problems and difficulty for him, however he went on to achieve some decent things for himself throughout his life, before turning to his life of death.

In the 1960's Gacy would become a self-made contractor, even going on to become the precinct captain of the Democratic Party in his Chicago suburb. Though he had a less than stellar childhood and didn't make friends easily, Gacy was well liked in adulthood and was known throughout the community. In fact, he was known as a clown at children's parties and an organizer of cultural gatherings within the community as well. His accomplishments were many, though he was married and divorced twice. Still, he went on to have many children of his own and still be liked by most around him.

Unfortunately, Gacy was hiding a dark secret. In approximately 1968 he is believed to have committed his first crime, sexually assaulting two teenage boys. He would go on to have a long history of crimes and jail sentences for a range of different sexual assault charges and more. But there was more going on and more soon to be going on that he didn't know about and that would definitely become a more pressing issue. Gacy would go on to commit over 30 murders while trying to assuage his homosexual thoughts.

According to Gacy he began murdering boys and men nearly every month after his divorce, taking them home with him to give them alcohol and drugs. Once he started watching movies with them he would handcuff and then strangle them. As time went on he continued to kidnap more and more children, drowning them, having sex with them and suffocating them. Some he would still strangle and a whole lot more, being careful to always take boys who would not be missed for some time and burying them under his house.

Over the course of 6 years Gacy continued to kidnap, torture, rape and kill a number of young teens and men but he would slowly become more adventurous and start taking bigger and bigger risks. The lack of risk involved in taking unknown children began to bore him, and he started taking boys from his own neighborhood, right down the street. Taking children right from the open and in front of others would come to be his biggest mistake and would be the thing that got him caught after all of his time killing undetected.

It was December 11th 1978 that Gacy picked up his last youth, Robert Piest. The two were seen having a conversation outside of a drug store and that would be the straw that broke the camels back for Gacy. The boy's mother became concerned when her son didn't return home and, since he had been the last one seen with the child, the police approached Gacy and even searched his house but couldn't find evidence of the boy. What they did find later was a roll of film that the boy had owned and later, three bodies in the crawl space. In fact, Gacy would go on to admit to the murders of these boys and would even inform police of where to find them.

At the time, however, police didn't even realize what they had found when they first found it. Executing a search warrant for the disappearance of Piest, police would search the crawl space and detect an awful smell, but would discount it as faulty sewage lines, not even questioning Gacy about the problem. They wouldn't realize their mistake until an evaluation of the items seized from the house was revealed to include a ring that had belonged to yet another missing boy. This led to a second search warrant and Gacy would go on to admit to police what he had done and even where to find all of the bodies, hoping that it would result in a lesser sentence.

John Wayne Gacy is believed to have committed his first murder in 1972 when he claims to have had sex with a boy who later attempted to attack him with a knife. When he got the knife away he killed the boy and buried him in the space under his garage. The next time he killed someone is unknown, but it's believed it was somewhere between 1972 and 1975 when he again kidnapped a boy and killed him before burying him under his basement. In 1976, things would escalate even further with his second divorce, leading to a total of over 30 murders.

Even worse, eight unidentified males would all be counted among his victims as well, and would be interred at eight different cemeteries. They remain unidentified even to this day and the families have no idea of what has happened to these young men. What's even worse still is that there may still have been additional victims of Gacy that were never found in any way and were never identified or claimed by Gacy himself. No one will ever know for sure.

In the end, Gacy would confess to 33 murders with 29 bodies found on his property and 4 found in a river nearby where he admitted to dumping them. Of course, once arrested, Gacy would recant his confession and would claim insanity, though he was unsuccessful in his plea. Instead, Gacy would go on to be sentenced to death. It would take a total of 14 years before he would actually fulfill his sentence, but he would spend those years at the Statesville Penitentiary.

On May 10, 1994, Gacy was executed by lethal injection.

Chapter III: The Green River Killer - Gary Ridgway

Gary Ridgway, also known as The Green River Killer, is known to have killed 70 people, though he was never convicted of all of them. Still, Ridgway was yet another quintessential example of what could happen to a child who suffered a terrible childhood. There was a little bit of everything going on in his life and though he would start out his high school and adult life in a completely normal manner, he would go on to become a serial murderer that no one would have expected, though they may have thought differently if they knew the childhood he came from.

Born in Salt Lake City, Utah in 1949, Gary Ridgway was the second child of Mary and Thomas Ridgway. His childhood was definitely not ideal as Ridgway argued constantly with his mother, often violently. Even more he continued bedwetting well into his teens and even tested with low intelligence. He was considered an embarrassment to his mother because of these things and its likely part of the reason that their arguments continued to be so violent.

Another explanation that has been touted many times is that Ridgway found himself sexually attracted to his mother and this led him to be embarrassed and angry as well. When it came to his father, however, Ridgway would hear a number of deviant stories about mortuary workers engaging in necrophilia. It's likely that this is where some of Ridgway's thoughts and actions actually came from. When combined with the difficulty that he had throughout this time of his life, it's definitely a sign of something.

Even though he struggled with a number of things from the bedwetting to fighting to low intelligence, Ridgway was actually very well-liked by his peers. They believed him to be congenial and friendly enough. In fact, most of them had no problem with him and he was able to make friends as a child. Still, he went on to attempt his first murder at the young age of 14, simply because he wanted to know what it would feel like to kill someone. He was unsuccessful, however, as the stab through the ribs did not kill the six-year-old boy that he had taken.

Ridgway would go on to marry his high school sweetheart and serve in the Vietnam War. While there he would go on to see a number of prostitutes. It's believed that he contracted gonorrhea from one of those prostitutes while he served in the Navy and this fed into his hatred of prostitutes. He would go on to marry two additional times and would continue to frequent prostitutes despite these thoughts and feelings of hatred. But it would likely be the beginning of his murderous thoughts and impulses during his life. His first murder would occur in 1982.

Gary Ridgway began his murder spree in 1982 with Wendy Coffield, a 16 year old girl who was a high school dropout and runaway. She was the beginning of a spree that would last for another nearly 10 years. In total, he would go on to kill at least 71 women and girls between the ages of 12 and 40, though he later stated that he had killed so many women that he actually lost count of all of them and couldn't remember much about them.

Starting in 1982 a slew of runaways and prostitutes began disappearing from the Route 99 area of King County, Washington. Ridgway would drive up and down the highway and would pick up a young woman, often showing them pictures of his son to get them to trust him and get in his truck. When they would agree to go with him he would kidnap them and take them to his house where he would rape each one and then strangle her from behind. Though he began by strangling each of the women by hand he realized quickly that they would leave marks on his arms as they attempted to defend themselves.

He believed that the cuts and bruises would make it easier for someone to identify him or would make people ask questions and so he began to use different types of ligatures to strangle the women. When he was finished with them he would take them to a secluded area where he would dispose of the bodies. In most instances the bodies were found grouped together and were often posed. Most of the women were also completely nude, but what authorities found most telling was the killer would return to the scene of the crime, not only to see it, but to have intercourse with the bodies.

In 1982 Ridgway was actually arrested on charges related to prostitution, but he was released soon after and no one was the wiser that he was actually involved in something far more serious. He became an official suspect in the Green River killings but was ruled out the following year when he passed a polygraph test. No one knew until much later that the quality standards for his test were far too lax and that he had actually failed the test. The FBI review conducted much later realized this after he was again a suspect.

Still, three years later the police would collect hair and saliva samples from Ridgway that would become his downfall. Of course, that wouldn't happen for quite some time as the DNA testing that was available at the time was simply not enough to detect from the bodies of the women that had been found. It was in the same year that the police contacted his wife, Judith Mawson, and discussed with her the possibility of his being the Green River Killer.

Judith and Ridgway had met and begun dating only two years before and they would be married the year after she was approached by authorities. She claimed to have no idea that her husband was committing murders when she believed him to be working overtime and also claimed that she had never even heard of the Green River Killer because she didn't like to watch the news. It would be a number of years before Ridgway would be arrested again, in 2001, for more prostitution charges. Later that year he would be arrested for the murders.

Along with 4 Jane Doe's and many possible victims who were never accounted for or claimed by Ridgway, there would be 48 women he would plead guilty to killing.

Ridgway was leaving work when he was arrested on suspicion of murder of four women. The women were the same ones he had been suspected of murdering nearly 20 years before but DNA evidence had finally caught up with what the police had been attempting all along. The saliva sample that Ridgway had given them conclusively matched the semen that was found on the victims and Ridgway was charged with the murders of Marcia Chapman, Opal Mills, Cynthia Hinds and Carol Ann Christensen. The police would add Wendy Coffield, Debra Bonner and Debra Estes after finding spray paint residue on them that matched what had been used in the factory where Ridgway worked.

A plea was entered of guilty, to 48 charges of aggravated first degree murder. The plea, along with information regarding locations of each of the remaining victims, would spare Gary Ridgway the death penalty. In January of 2004, Ridgway was placed in solitary confinement and in 2015 he was sent to a High Security Federal Prison in Colorado.

Gary Ridgway remains in prison to this day for 49 consecutive life sentences, handed down for each of the 49 murders he plead guilty to as well as 49 counts of tampering with evidence.

Chapter IV: BTK - Dennis Rader

Also known as the BTK killer of Bind, Torture, Kill, Dennis Rader seemed to have a completely normal youth and even adulthood. He was a relatively normal child and seemed to have no problem with his youth. He was born in Kansas in 1945 as the eldest of four sons. His parents, William and Dorothea, had him baptized and raised him in what seemed to be a normal fashion, but no one could know what he would go on to do as he grew older.

As a child, Dennis Rader seemed entirely ordinary. He was a Boy Scout and a participant in church youth group events. He was an average student and though he seemed a little bit withdrawn, he didn't have a lot of outwardly odd tendencies or signs that something was wrong. His family life was quite normal and those who knew him best thought that he was quite quiet and polite. Though he was withdrawn and they noticed, no one seemed to think this was strange and most still felt he was an average child. They didn't know what was under the surface.

Rader admits that he actually started developing fantasies about binding and torturing girls when he first started to reach puberty. He started to dream about tying girls up and doing what he wanted with them but knew that these kinds of thoughts needed to be kept secret. He became quite adept at keeping this secret from others and managed to do some long after he started killing. At the same time he was also killing small animals like dogs and cats, hanging them until they died. No one knew of any of these things about him until he finally admitted them during his testimony to police.

When he got older Rader entered college and seemed, by all accounts, to be focused on success. He was soft-spoken and worked hard for his own support from his high school years onward. Though he tried to become more extroverted he was not successful and it seems he was beginning his first trolling for victims during this time. Though this isn't known for sure, his journals and accounts seem to indicate it.

Not only that but he began his other crimes at the time, beginning with burglary and breaking and entering.

Somewhere around age 21 Rader decided to join the Air Force and spent four years on basic tasks with average advancements. He began seeing prostitutes at this time and though he wanted to engage in bondage, they weren't interested. He would stalk victims at this time but never pursued any kind of aggressive behavior beyond the stalking. His friends and coworkers would all describe him as a normal guy. When he returned home, Rader got married and seemed to have a normal life. It was when he lost his job and was killing time driving his wife to and from work that everything changed.

It was January of 1974 when Dennis Rader killed his very first victim. In fact, he killed an entire family in their own home. Prior to this he had stalked a number of women, especially after losing his job, but he had never injured or attempted to approach any of them until he noticed Julie Otero. He claimed he was obsessed with Hispanic women and when he found Julie and her daughter Josephine he began to stalk them. It took a while before he worked up the intent to actually interact with them and to break into their home with the intent to attack the woman and her two children, but things went wrong from the start.

Mr. Otero was home that day and Rader had not expected this. He had a gun with him however and used it to keep some semblance of control over the situation. He tied everyone up in the bedroom claimed to have tried to make each of them more comfortable, especially Mr. Otero as he had suffered a cracked rib from a car accident. It was while they were pressing him to take their car and whatever money they had that he realized he would have to kill them because they would be able to easily identify him. It began with the father.

Rader put a plastic bag over the husbands head and wrapped cords around his neck to strangle him, but he didn't die so he strangled him a second time, this time with a t-shirt or cloth. Rader then went on to the wife, strangling her until she passed out and proceeding to the daughter and the son. But Mrs. Otero woke up again and Rader had to strangle her again. This time she did not wake up but her son did. So Rader took the boy to another room and covered his head with a cloth and the bag and killed him this time. When Josephine also woke up, however, he took her into the basement and hung her.

It was the first of his murders, but it would definitely not be the last, as Rader would go on to kill six more people over a period of nearly 20 years. His crimes, being reasonably thought out and executed could possibly have gone on were it not for one very important detail, his own hubris. Dennis Rader wanted everyone to know what he did and he wanted all of them to know about the kill. It was after his second murder that Rader attempted to contact someone, writing a letter that he left in a book at the library to take credit for the Otero murders. It was in this letter that he named himself.

In March and then December of 1977, Rader killed yet again but after the December killing of Nancy Fox he reported the crime to police. He followed this up with a poem about his next murder in the following month and then sent a letter to a local news station about the latest three murders that he had committed, but even with the letters, no one was able to connect Dennis Rader to the crimes. No one was even looking for him. After all, Dennis Rader seemed to be an excellent husband and father. He attended Wichita State University and got a degree in the administration of justice and he continued to kill whenever he found the time.

For the next several years Rader killed sparingly, once waiting in an elderly woman's home and then leaving before she even arrived. Two other times he killed near his own home, but no one really knows why he decided to stop killing after the murder of Dolores Davis in 1991. It was in this same year that he became a Park City compliance supervisor and became extremely strict about the rules. He became a Boy Scout leader and was extremely active in the church but in 2004, things started to unravel quickly as his hubris finally became his undoing.

10 total victims and 2 survivors actually make Rader one of the least 'accomplished' of the killers in this book.

It was throughout 2004 and 2005; Rader began sending letters to the authorities and the news outlets. He would send pictures of victims, word puzzles and even outlines of his own story. He would leave packages with clues and, in the one that sealed everything, a floppy disk. That disk led them back to the church and images of his white van on security camera footage led them even closer to him. With a DNA sample from his daughter they were finally able to close the case and Dennis Rader was arrested on February 25, 2005.

Everyone around Rader was completely shocked by the news and couldn't believe that he could be responsible for 10 murders. But only 4 months later Rader would plead guilty to all of the charges as part of a plea agreement. In exchange, Rader would give all of the details about his crimes, never once showing remorse or any type of guilt over them. As the death penalty had been abolished in the state at the time of his crimes, Rader was sentenced to 10 life sentences.

Rader is currently still incarcerated in a Kansas prison, serving his 10 life sentences for first degree murder.

Chapter V: Son of Sam – David Berkowitz

David Berkowitz, also known as the .44 Caliber Killer and, more commonly, the Son of Sam, lived an idyllic life in New York City. He was one of those who no one would have imagined would go on to such a horrible life because everything about his childhood seemed absolutely perfect and exactly what any child could have wanted. But later he would become one of the most well-known and horrific killers in the country, with a death toll of 6 and a list of wounded even longer.

Berkowitz was born in 1953 in New York City, the child of Betty Broder and Joseph Kleinman. Both of them being poor and his father being less than thrilled with the idea of raising him, he was put up for adoption where he was quickly taken in by Nathan and Pearl Berkowitz. The two doted on their child and gave him everything he could possibly want in his childhood, caring for him and doing everything they could to make his life easier, though they weren't sure what to do about some of his tendencies.

Berkowitz was a loner from his childhood, finding it difficult to make friends and interact with others. They would describe him as hyperactive, aggressive, isolated and even violent. His parents had no idea what to do about these actions and though they attempted to do everything they could for him, he was a bully to other children. Still, his parents continued to work at making his life easier, until his mother passed away while he was still a teenager. Berkowitz found himself developing a range of mental issues and problems while trying to deal with the loss.

It is believed at this time that he started feeling paranoia and self-persecution. His father remarried during this time and Berkowitz found himself falling deeper and deeper into his isolation and self-delusion. Still, he joined the army and became an excellent marksman, something that he would carry on when he began killing a number of years later. This was 1971 and Berkowitz was only 18 years old. He would later claim that he had contacted his biological mother and she rejected him, leading to his feelings of resentment, however evidence indicates that his mother instead welcomed him and their connection. It was Berkowitz who ended the relationship.

His first sexual encounter was during his time in the Army and Berkowitz developed an STD from the prostitute that he was with. It was with this event that he began to feel even angrier, especially towards women. He also began setting fires during this time, creating several hundred throughout the area. But his hatred for women led him in a different direction and it wasn't long before Berkowitz was looking for more than a fire.

The Son of Sam killer began terrorizing the city of New York in December of 1975 and though his reign would be a short one, lasting just over 1 year he would go on to kill 6 people and injure 7 more. His first murder would occur when he killed two women with a hunting knife on Christmas Eve. It would be his second murder that would lead to his using a .44 caliber bulldog handgun. And this murder would also involve two different people, though only one of them would be killed.

Donna Lauria and Jody Valenti were sitting in a car when Berkowitz walked up to them and opened fire. The crime was simple and he merely fired three shots into the vehicle before calmly walking away again. Lauria was dead immediately while her friend survived, but was unable to give enough of a description to actually find the man responsible. Still, her witness statement was corroborated by another witness, the other victim's father, who had seen the same man sitting in a car nearby.

It would be three months before Berkowitz attacked again. Once again he would go after two individuals sitting in their vehicle but this time he would succeed in killing neither of them. Instead, he fired off several shots and shattered the windshield of the vehicle. The two in the car, Carl Denaro and Rosemary Keenan, would not even realize they had been shot at until they drove away and realized Denaro had a bullet in his head. Both would survive and though police managed to identify the bullet type, they did not identify the gun. Nor did they connect the shooting with the previous one.

One month later two more girls would be attacked, though this time they were sitting on a porch when a man walked up to them and took out a revolver. One of the girls would be paralyzed from the incident, while the other would be virtually unharmed over the long term. Once again, there was a sketch made and there were witnesses, but other than the .44 caliber bullets, little was known about the suspect. It was the following year, though only two months later that the next victims were attacked. And three months again before the next one would be. Virginia Voskerichian was the only victim to be attacked while she was alone and she would be the second to die from her wound. His next two victims would also die, before they could speak to the police.

It was with these latest victims, killed in April of 1977 that Berkowitz would first attempt to interact with police. Giving himself the name 'Son of Sam, Berkowitz addressed his letter to the captain of the police department and stated that he would continue to kill. It was finally time for the police to start connecting the dots and recognizing the link between each of the previous crimes. This would, however, only be the first time that Berkowitz would attempt to contact police and the media about his crimes.

Police determined that the shooter was likely neurotic and paranoid schizophrenic, but they were unable to determine who it was that owned the gun, even after tracking down every legally owned and registered .44

caliber Bulldog. Berkowitz himself would contact the media two months later, calling out the police for their inability to catch them. Two more couples would be shot in their vehicles over the remaining few months and witness descriptions continued to speak of a blonde or brown haired man of stocky build. But they also recognized a yellow car.

There would be 6 murder victims of Berkowitz in total and 7 survivors.

Initially the police believed Berkowitz to be a witness to the crime, but in August of 1977 they performed an unauthorized search of his car and found maps from the crime scenes, and a Son of Sam letter that had never been sent. When he left his apartment they found him with a paper bag holding his

.44 Bulldog and never had to worry about him denying the charges. In fact, he asked the police why it took such a long time to find him.

In the house they found graffiti and diaries that discussed a range of arsons that he claimed to have set throughout the state. When they began questioning him he immediately confessed to each of the killings and injuries, claiming that his former neighbors' dog was possessed by a demon and the demon had told him to kill. It was only alter that he would admit the demon possession story was a hoax and that there had never been anyone telling him to kill.

Berkowitz was sentenced to 25 years for each of the 6 murders and is currently incarcerated at the Sullivan Correctional Facility.

Chapter VI: The Hillside Stranglers – Kenneth Bianchi & Angelo Buono Jr.

Not much would have suggested that Kenneth Bianchi and Angelo Buono Jr., two cousins who were born in different parts of the country in only mildly dysfunctional homes, would go on to become The Hillside Stranglers, raping and killing as many as 10 women and girls in only a four month period. But circumstances threw them together and each seemed to build on the bad about the other until … well history definitely knows the rest.

Kenneth Bianchi had a less than stellar upbringing, but it still wasn't what one would have expected for a serial killer. His mother was an alcoholic prostitute who gave birth to him in 1951. Unable or unwilling to care for him, Bianchi's mother gave him up within two weeks of his birth and he was adopted into the Bianchi family (a possible name at birth is not known). But Bianchi was not the idyllic child from the start, being a compulsive liar. He was diagnosed with petit mal seizures due to his tendency to fall into a trance at random times and was also diagnosed with an involuntary urination disorder and passive-aggressive personality disorder. Still, he was tested with above average intelligence.

Though he was smart, Bianchi was a classic underachiever and didn't get along well with his teachers. His mother and teachers all agreed that he was lazy and wasn't working hard at keeping up with his studies or his peers. When his adoptive father died in his teen years, Bianchi had no signs of grief but his mother was forced to go back to work to support the family. Bianchi would go on to marry his high school sweetheart, though the relationship was doomed to fail even from the start and lasted only eight months. It was sometime after this that he started working odd jobs as he could never get the job he wanted as a police officer.

Starting a job as a security guard instead, Bianchi began stealing valuable items from the jewelry store that he worked at and would give them away to his girlfriends or to prostitutes. Unfortunately, these crimes meant he had to keep on the move and in 1977 he moved to Los Angeles to live with his adoptive cousin, starting as pimps and quickly escalating to murder.

Born in 1934, Buono had a relatively normal childhood until he was five years old and his parents divorced. At this point, he was taken to Glendale with his mother and sister. Always brutal and angry towards women, at the age of only 14 Buono started using demeaning terms for his mother and referring to sodomizing and raping girls to his friends. He was already committing larceny and was caught and sent to a reform school at the age of 16.

His first child was born when Buono was only 17 and he married the mother, only to leave her a short time later. He married again and had another five children with a second wife by the time he was 28-years-old. It's believed his crimes even continued to the point of raping his youngest child and only daughter at this time. It's known that he was still committing petty theft and refusing to pay child support. He was also known to be extremely violent towards his wife, even in front of their children. She filed for divorce and he moved in with another woman a short time later.

His brutality towards women is well-known and it is believed the women thought they would be killed if they left. His third wife had two children of his but when he began bragging about raping her daughter and even letting his sons get in on it she decided to run away. Buono chose to marry again, though he never lives with his final wife. Instead, he goes on to commit assault and force women to perform sex acts with him, even having sex with the girlfriends of his may sons. It's around this time that his cousin, Kenneth Bianchi, came to live with the family.

It was 1977 when Bianchi and Buono first started their life in crime. Bianchi would often bring home prostitutes and they began to discuss the likelihood of anyone missing one of the women if they went missing. In October, this led them to rape and strangles their very first victim, Yolanda Washington. It took only a month for them to attack another three prostitutes, picking them up in a van and bringing them back to their house.

Each of the women was sexually assaulted in many different ways before being tortured and then strangled. Careful to avoid detection, the two men would scrub the bodies carefully before taking them to the hillside and disposing of them. They would leave the women in extremely provocative positions, generally nearby a police station being completely convinced they would never be caught. The crimes began to be attributed to the Hillside Strangler, because of the location each of the bodies was discovered in, but no one realized that more than one man was responsible.

Other victims were teenage runaways and prostitutes who were each younger women and teens, including Judy Miller, Elissa Kastin and Jill Barcomb. But a high school student and two younger girls would be the next three victims. The search for the Hillside Strangler began to intensify as the girls being hunted were no longer those at-risk, but instead were vulnerable children and girls. It was some time after another victim was found that police finally started to consider the idea of a partnership.

Even more, police actually interviewed Bianchi, as he lived in the same apartment complex as one of the victims, but didn't consider him a suspect at the time. Four more victims would be found, with one being older than the others, before the two men would go their separate ways.

It took approximately a year for the two to have a falling out and it was exacerbated by the fact that Bianchi wanted to reconcile with his girlfriend, who had moved to Washington. The two men had killed 10 women in this period of time and Bianchi was welcomed to Washington to make things work with his girlfriend. After failing to get a job as a police officer, he would become a security guard and attempt to assimilate into normal life. But Bianchi couldn't simply turn off the impulse to kill and his first solo murder, that of two college girls, would be the one that got both of the men caught.

The two women were seen by witnesses with Bianchi and when the witness came forward it didn't take long for the police to arrest him. Even more, the girls had been set up to come to his house under the guise of a housesitting job and had written a note about the meeting that was found in their car. Attempting to get away with the crime under a plea of insanity, Bianchi claimed that he had a split personality disorder and that another of his personalities had committed the murders. Unfortunately for him, it didn't take long for professionals to see through the ruse and determine that he was perfectly sane. He then decided to turn the tables on his ex-partner.

Bianchi confessed to all of the murders attributed to the Hillside Strangler and in order to avoid the death penalty he also turned in Buono. Buono, of course, was a little sneakier than had been expected and it was difficult at first for the investigators to pin anything on him. The murder scenes were clean, as were the victims themselves and in Buono's house they could find nothing that would tie him to the murders or anything else. In fact, there wasn't even evidence that it was his house as no fingerprints of any kind could be found. It would take witnesses to convict him, and witnesses they definitely had. Over 400 eventually testified along with Bianchi and Buono was found guilty of nine murders.

Angelo Buono was sentenced to life without parole but died of a heart attack in 2002. Bianchi remains in prison to this day.

Chapter VII: Milwaukee Cannibal - Jeffrey Dahmer

Perhaps no serial killers name strikes fear in anyone more than Jeffrey Dahmer. Even those who don't really know much about what he did or who he was have likely heard the name and there's something about it that you just don't forget. Known as the Milwaukee Cannibal, Jeffrey Dahmer was most definitely psychopathic enough to make it onto this list of the most evil of them all. His murder count may have been lower than some of the others, at 17, but the things he did to those people (before and after their death) definitely mean something.

Starting his life with a perfectly normal childhood, Jeffrey Dahmer was the eldest child of Lionel and Joyce Dahmer. He seemed to be a happy and energetic child and no one who knew him in those days would have ever suspected what he would someday become. It wasn't until he was four years old and had to undergo surgery for a double hernia that he seemed to change, almost overnight. The happy-go-lucky child was gone and Dahmer began to withdraw further into himself, a fact that compounded when his younger brother was born and the family began to move constantly.

When he was 8 years old Dahmer was sexually assaulted by a boy in his neighborhood. The crime was never reported but it most definitely changed the way that Dahmer saw himself and the world that he lived in. He felt that he was no longer safe in his own life and within two years he was experimenting with dead animals, decapitating them, bleaching bones, nailing a carcass to a tree and a whole lot more. Though his parents were somewhat concerned they saw the actions as their son being just a normal boy and largely ignored them.

By the time Dahmer reached his teen years he was entirely disengaged in life and seemed tense. He had difficulty making friends and was generally friendless and alone. By his own admission he began to turn toward thoughts of necrophilia and murder when he was about this age, but he never acted on them until things in the rest of his family seemed to start breaking down even further, where his parents divorced following a period of intense fighting that seemed to emotionally scar Dahmer for the rest of his life.

His short temper and strange speech patterns made it difficult for Dahmer to fit in, but he would seek ways to draw attention in a positive way even still. As a result, Dahmer began drinking to try and fit in with his fellow students. An average student himself, Jeffrey felt left out entirely when, upon his parents' divorce, there was no interest in what would happen to him. Because he was 18, his parents only cared about their younger son and when his mother took the boy and left town, Dahmer's father left him behind in the house they had once shared. Things would only get worse from there.

The murders began in 1978, when Dahmer was 18 years old. The victim was another 18-year-old, a hitchhiker that Dahmer picked up on the road and brought back for some partying and drinking. After a couple of hours Seven Hicks wanted to leave, but Dahmer, being unwilling to let him go, proceeded to beat him over the head with a dumbbell. Hicks fell unconscious but Dahmer wasn't done, strangling him with the bar from the dumbbell until he was dead.

It was after this that he stripped the boy of his clothes and masturbated over him. The following day he decided to dissect the body, beginning a slew of experiments that would occur over the next several weeks with Hicks' body. He would bury the remains in a grave before pulling them up again and pulling flesh from bone before dissolving it in acid and flushing it down the toilet. The bones he would crush into small pieces with a sledgehammer and scatter throughout the woods of the family home. No one would ever realize what he had done.

Instead, Dahmer would head off to university and then the army, where he was accused later of having raped two young men who served with him. Though he was considered a good soldier at the start, Dahmer began to deteriorate fast and was eventually deemed unsuitable for the military. He was released, but as his superiors believed his actions would not be a problem in his civilian life, nothing was done about them or even reported. Dahmer was allowed to return to anywhere he wanted in the states and chose Miami Beach. It was 1981 before he returned to Ohio.

Over the next several years Dahmer would be arrested on various charges from drunk and disorderly to indecent exposure. It was not long after this, in 1985, that he began to fall into more fantasies about control and dominance, beginning to experiment with gay bars, bookstores and even bathhouses. Later in the year he was visiting bathhouses frequently, but the idea of moving and responding partners was not something Dahmer was interested in and he began giving his partners sleeping pills instead, before raping them while they were unconscious. It was November of 1987 before he killed again.

Dahmer had taken a willing young man back to his hotel room and intended only to drug and rape the man. When he awoke in the morning however, the man was obviously dead with his chest crushed and blood coming out of his moth. Though Dahmer could not remember killing him, he took the body home in a large suitcase and began dismembering the body. When he was finished he threw out the pieces except for the head, keeping it wrapped in a blanket before he boiled it and kept the skull for his own pleasure. It was after this that Dahmer began to kill his victims.

The encounter would start with Dahmer bringing home willing men who he would render unconscious before raping and then killing them. Strangulation became his method of choice for killing the victims and after killing each he would dismember the corpse into small pieces that could easily be disposed of. It was his fifth victim, 24-year-old Anthony Sears that Dahmer would decide to keep. He disposed of the majority of the victim but retained his head and genitalia, storing them in his locker at work and taking them with him when he moved.

He would kill another 12 men before finally being caught. In fact, it would be because he lost his concentration for a moment that he would be finally caught as his final intended victim, Tracy Edwards, managed to escape from his apartment during his ritual.

It was 11:30 at night when Edwards managed to get out of the apartment and flag down police. When the police couldn't get the handcuffs off the man he agreed to take them back to the apartment to get the keys. The three were allowed into the home and Edwards revealed that a large knife had been brandished at him as well. The men were instructed that the key to the handcuffs was in the bedroom and all of them went to the room where the officers saw the large knife under the bed.

Officers also saw an open drawer containing pictures that Dahmer had taken of decomposing and dismembered bodies. When he looked at the pictures closer, the officer was able to see that they were in fact real and immediately proceeded to arrest Dahmer, who began to fight as soon as he saw the officer with the pictures. He was cuffed and officers finally looked in his fridge, seeing the severed head of one of his victims on the shelf. While going through the apartment four severed heads and seven skulls were found along with two human hearts and a range of other organs, muscles, body parts and a whole lot more. The pictures would provide a great deal of evidence of who the men were and how many had once been there.

It was July 23, 1991 when Dahmer was first questioned and it would take two weeks for the entire interrogation to be completed. Dahmer waived his right to an attorney and admitted to all 17 murders with 16 in Wisconsin and one in Ohio. He admitted to necrophilia and also admitted to consuming organs and even some of the muscles of several of his victims, a fact that has made him one of the most well-known serial killers in the country. He would be charged with all 17 murders by the end of September. The trial began only three months later and Dahmer pled guilty to all counts.

Dahmer was sentenced to 1 count of life in prison, 2 counts of life plus 10 years and 13 counts of life plus 70 years. He was beaten by a fellow inmate, Christopher Scarver, on November 28, 1994, dying an hour later from the injuries.

Chapter VIII: The Co-Ed Killer - Edmund Kemper

The Co-Ed Killer plagued the California area in the 1970's before eventually turning himself in, but his reasoning for killing may be one of the most chilling of them all; he simply wanted to know what it would feel like. Starting out his childhood with mental problems, Kemper definitely didn't have a normal childhood and never was someone that his mother or anyone else in the family would trust. It was just a matter of time before something would happen to turn this disturbing child into something far worse.

Known as The Co-Ed Killer in his later life, Kemper started life as the middle child of E.E. and Clarnell Kemper. When his parents divorced while he was only 9 he was taken to live with his mother and sisters in Montana. His mother, an alcoholic, was never close with Edmund and was extremely critical of everything he did. Because of this, he was extremely critical of her, blaming every shortcoming he had on her treatment of him. Within just a year of moving with the family, his mother became frightened of what he might do to the rest of them.

Believing he might harm his sisters, his mother would force Edmund to live in the basement of their home, away from the rest of the family. This may have been before or after he began dreaming about disturbing events such as the death and mutilation of his family. He would cut the heads off his sister's dolls and would pretend to be killed in a gas chamber, a game he shared with his sisters and which disturbed all of them even more. What was worse, however, was when he was found to have buried alive the family cat.

Three years later Kemper would commit his first brutal murder of the second family cat, using a knife to slaughter the thing. He was sent to live with his father for a short while and then back to his mother. However, when she was unable to take care of him he was finally sent to live with his father's parents back in California. It would be a huge mistake that led him faster down the path of evil and destruction. A strange child already who would kill birds and other animals, he felt pinned down by his grandparent's rules and their refusal to let him have a gun. Their deaths would be the first human ones he would take at the young age of 15.

When he reported the murder to his mother and later to the police he would claim he simply wanted to know what it felt like. It would be the beginning of a long history in and out of facilities. An extremely smart child with a high IQ, Kemper was nonetheless diagnosed with paranoid schizophrenia and kept in a state hospital until he turned 21. His dream was to be a state trooper, however his size got him rejected and he was forced to make his way in a series of odd jobs. Unable to hold down a job after an injury, Kemper would get bored and begin picking up hitchhikers as he drove around in his car. It would be the beginning of the end.

Known as The Co-Ed Killer, Edmund Kemper was ultimately charged with killing 10 people and served time for each of the murders. His first killings were actually of his grandparents, who he felt had stifled him in what he wanted and were not allowing him to live his life. He later claimed that he killed his grandmother simply because he wanted to know what it would feel like to kill someone. After she was dead he killed his grandfather before he could come into the house, stating that he didn't want his grandfather to know that she was dead.

Kemper would serve time in a juvenile home for the murders of his grandparents and would go on to live a somewhat normal life on the outside for several years. It was much later that he suffered the motorcycle accident and was unable to work. At this point he would drive around for extended periods of time and would pick up a number of female hitchhikers. By his own accounts he picked up over 150 that he would simply let go when they had reached their destination, but in May of 1972, everything changed.

It started with two college students hitchhiking but there were a number of other women after this. He would pick up the women under the pretense of getting them where they wanted to go, but when he had them in his vehicle he would instead take them to an isolated spot. His method of choice for murdering the women was different between different murders but by turns he shot, stabbed, smothered and strangled the women that he kidnapped.

Their dead bodies he would bring to his home where he would perform sex acts on them before dissecting and dismembering them.

Mary Ann Pesce and Anita Luchessa were the first victims, both 18 and hitchhiking to Stanford University. He drove them around for approximately an hour before he found a secluded spot to kill them. He handcuffed the Pesce and made sure to lock Luchessa away in the trunk so that he could kill the women separately. With the two bodies in the trunk he was even stopped by a police officer for a broken taillight, but managed to get by without detection for the murders. The bodies were disposed of in plastic bags near Loma Prieta Mountain, though the pieces other than Mary Ann's skull were never found.

There were a total of four additional victims before Kemper would finally go after his mother. He eventually fell asleep waiting for her to arrive at home and when she did he allowed her to fall asleep before killing her with a claw hammer and a knife. After this he engaged in sexual acts with her body and decapitated head, throwing darts and screaming at her before cutting her tongue and larynx out of her body and putting them through the garbage disposal. He later invited his mother's friend to the house before killing her as well. He left a note at the house about the crime and drove off but it wasn't long before he decided to call in the murders.

Edmund Kemper reported the murders to the police from a pay phone and actually confessed to killing his mother and her best friend but police believed the call to be a hoax. When he called back several hours later he spoke to an officer that he knew and again confessed to the murders. Police arrived a short time later to arrest him and he confessed to all of the murders he had committed. He claimed that there was no further reason for him to run or for him to commit more murders and so; he decided to end it all.

Kemper was found guilty on all charges after giving an extremely detailed confession to everything he had done, including cooking and eating parts of his victims. On November 8, 1973, Kemper was finally declared guilty and set to be sentenced. Though he asked for the death penalty, there was a moratorium on capital punishment and he was instead sentenced to life.

Kemper is currently serving 8 consecutive sentences of 7 years to life with the possibility of parole again in 2017. (He has twice been eligible for parole and told the board that he was not fit to return to society.)

Over an 11 month period he murdered a total of five co-eds and a high school student before turning the tables and going back after someone he knew. In this case, it was his mother and her best friend. Many, including Kemper himself and his psychiatrists, believed that the women he killed were simply surrogates for his mother, who he would often be fighting with when he went out hunting for the women. When he did finally kill her he committed a number of humiliating acts to her corpse that are believed to substantiate this belief.

Chapter IX: The Tool Box Killers – Lawrence Bittaker & Roy Norris

If these two men hadn't met in prison it's likely they would have continued on a dangerous track of their own but when the two of them did meet, it was the start of something even more horrendous. Normal childhoods led to something terrible in their lives and five young women were the victims who paid the price. But what could possibly have happened in the lives of these two young men to turn them into killers? No one really knows and it's likely that we never will.

Adopted shortly after his birth, Lawrence was raised by George Bittaker and his wife after his biological parents gave him away. His early life was quite normal and seemed destined to continue until he started getting into trouble with the law. Arrested for shoplifting at the age of 12, he continued to end up in and out of jail and juvenile courts for additional shoplifting and petty theft charges. By his own account these actions were a result of lack of love from his parents, but it was never certain that was the case.

Before he graduated from high school Bittaker would drop out, even though his IQ of 138 said that he should be an excellent student. Instead, Bittaker found the entire experience boring and tedious. Within one year of dropping out he would be arrested for car theft, evading arrest and a hit and run. His crimes would land him in the California Youth Authority for the rest of the year until he turned 18. At that point, he was released from jail, but found that he no longer had any parents at all as his adoptive ones had disowned him and moved away.

Bittaker continued committing a range of different crimes and was eventually diagnosed as being highly manipulative. He would be diagnosed also as borderline psychotic and would claim that he couldn't control his compulsion to commit crimes. Finding himself in and out of jail for burglary, theft and more, it would be 1974 when he was first committed to prison for the attempted murder of a store clerk. It was there that he would meet Roy Norris in California Men's Colony.

Roy Norris was born in 1948 to a drug addicted mother. Though his parents married to keep the illegitimacy of his birth a secret, he would constantly be taken away from the home to stay in foster care. Always kept in Colorado, Norris would feel wronged throughout his childhood because he was wrongfully accused of various things while with his parents and was neglected by most of his foster families. He would later claim to have been sexually assaulted by a Hispanic foster family, which he claimed fueled his racism.

He was 16 when he first attempted to take his own life by injecting air into his arteries following a sexually explicit conversation with a relative. When his father was notified and threatened to beat him, Norris attempted to kill himself but was apprehended and sent back home. It was at this time that his parents informed him and his sister that they had never wanted either of them and intended to divorce. Norris dropped out of high school shortly after and joined the Navy, serving in Vietnam though he never saw any active combat.

Norris was 21 when he was arrested for the first in a string of sexual assault charges. Diagnosed with severe schizoid personality by the military after several attempts to sexually assault women, he was released with psychological problems. After spending several years in and out of jail and prison for assaults and rape Norris was declared to no longer be a danger to others and released. It took him only three months to offend again and one more month to be arrested and sent to the California Men's Colony.

The two men who would come to be known as The Toolbox Killers met when they spent time together in the California Men's Colony where Bittaker managed to save Norris' life on two separate occasions. They started to discuss their crimes and while Norris mentioned that he was stimulated by frightened women, Bittaker mentioned that he would kill a woman if he ever raped her so there would be no witness. The two began to discuss their plans to meet after their release to rape and kill teenage girls, being determined to kill one between the years of 13 and 19.

Bittaker was released in 1978 and managed to get a job where he made friends and was well liked. He even donated to The Salvation Army and would bring teenagers back to his apartment for beer and marijuana. Three months later, Norris was released and the two met to again discuss their plans. Everything was still just as they had planned and they were agreed to start the process of abducting girls for themselves. They purchased a large cargo van to make the process easier and began to pick up female hitchhikers in February of 1979. Though none of these women were ever assaulted, the two considered these to be practice runs to figure out how to abduct women.

They managed to find a secluded road where they could bring the women and so began their first venture into killing. It was June of 1979 and they drove down toward the beach. They attempted to pick up Lucinda Schaefer but she refused to go with them so they had to improvise. Instead of luring her into the vehicle they abducted her when she was away from others and then drove down the road to their hidden place. Bittaker kept the radio up so no one could hear her while Norris bound and gagged her for the trip.

Each of the men raped her alternately and commented on how the girl never offered any kind of resistance or even cried during the attack. Instead, she merely asked if they were going to kill her and if she could be allowed to pray before they did if that was their intent. The men argued about whether or not to kill her before they actually did before Norris attempted to strangle her. When he did, however, he was disturbed by the look he received from her and ran away, leaving Bittaker to strangle her first with his hands and then with a wire hanger. She was wrapped in a shower curtain and thrown over a canyon.

The following victims were each tormented, raped and strangled before being tossed over the side of cliffs, chasms and canyons to dispose of their bodies. There were only five victims of the Toolbox Killers, however the horrific ways in which they sexually assaulted and mutilated their victims including using pliers, ice picks and more, most definitely caused them to be named in this list of the worst serial killers around. The two men continued their torture with 18-year-old Andrea Hall, who was hitchhiking, as well as 13-year-old Jacqueline Lamp and 15-year-old Jackie Gilliam and 16-year-old Shirley Ledford.

Shirley would be the last victim that they would kill and she would suffer a great deal of torture from a sledgehammer and pliers as well as wire coat hanger before finally being dumped, dead, on a random lawn. The two men determined that they wanted to see a reaction from the press and so, Shirley Ledford was discovered in that lawn the following morning. She was the one who suffered seemingly the most, though each of the victims was brutally attacked. It would be their own hubris that would get them caught, however, as Norris decided to share their exploits with another criminal in November of 1979.

When Norris revealed to Jimmy Dalton the crimes they had committed he eventually decided to turn them over to the police who immediately noticed the similarity between crimes that had been reported and missing teenage girls and rape accusations where there had been no arrests and the details that Dalton had been told by Norris. When the mug shots of Bittaker and Norris were presented to one of the surviving rape victims she easily identified the two as the men who had taken her. Norris would first be arrested for dealing marijuana, a charge police were able to pin on him after a period of surveillance. Bittaker was arrested for the rape the same day. The two men ended up held for parole violations however, as the rape victim was unable to identify them in person.

When the apartments and vehicles were searched however, police would find a great deal of evidence placing them with the victims including jewelry, tools, photographs and a whole lot more. It was November 1979 still when Norris was first presented with the facts of the cases against him. At first he continued to deny the facts and the crimes but when too much evidence continued to point his way he tried to turn all the blame on Bittaker, portraying him as the mastermind behind everything. It was 1980 before the two men were charged with the murders and this after Norris successfully led police to two of the bodies. Norris agreed to a plea bargain where he would testify against his former partner in exchange for the removal of the death penalty and life without parole from any possibility.

Norris was sentenced to 45 years to life in 1980 and remains in Donovan State Prison to this day. Lawrence Bittaker is currently on death row at San Quentin State Prison.

Conclusion

Serial killers live throughout the country and around the world. At any given time it is not even known how many serial killers may live among us or even be hunting among us, but it is definitely a good thing to know that even one of them will never again walk the earth. With these 11 serial killers there is still the possibility that a few may someday be released, though the likelihood, even when they are offered the possibility of parole, is extremely small. With the level of brutality, horror and cruelty in the kills that each of these men has created, it's extremely unlikely that any parole board will see fit to release them.

The best thing for all of those involved was the sentencing of each of these men and those who currently await their death in a prison cell or on death row have nothing left but to give jailhouse interviews and confess to the crimes they have committed. Each of the men here has, in some way or another, confessed to the crimes that they have committed whether they have confessed to all or only a few of the actual murders. But each one has a reason for being listed in this compilation of some of the most evil and psychopathic killers of all time.

Printed in Great
Britain
by Amazon